other books by Francis A. Schaeffer

Francis A. Schaeffer

The Mark
of the
Christian

InterVarsity Press
Downers Grove
Illinois 60515

© 1970 by L'Abri Fellowship

All rights reserved. No part of this book may be reproduced in any form without written permission from InterVarsity Press, P.O. Box 1400, Downers Grove, Illinois 60515.

InterVarsity Press® is the book-publishing division of InterVarsity Christian Fellowship®, a student movement active on campus at hundreds of universities, colleges and schools of nursing in the United States of America, and a member movement of the International Fellowship of Evangelical Students. For information about local and regional activities, write Public Relations Dept., InterVarsity Christian Fellowship, 6400 Schroeder Rd., P.O. Box 7895, Madison, WI 53707-7895.

ISBN 0-87784-434-8

Printed in the United States of America

33	32	31	30	29	28	27	26	25
04	03	02	01	00	99	98		

foreword

Christians have not always presented a pretty picture to the world. Too often they have failed to show the beauty of love, the beauty of Christ, the holiness of God.

And the world has turned away.

Is there then no way to make the world look again—this time at true Christianity? Must Christians continue to stand with arms folded, going on in their old sweet ways, presenting to men a tarnished image of God—a shattered body of Christ?

Francis A. Schaeffer meets these questions head-on.

This small book was originally intended solely as a part of a longer work—*The Church at the End of the 20th Century*. But the message of this essay is so significant that we feel it should take its place alongside *Escape from Reason, The God Who Is There, Death in the City* and *The Church at the End of the 20th Century*.

To conclude the book the author has chosen "Lament," an appropriate poem by Evangeline Paterson.

—the publisher

THE MARK OF THE CHRISTIAN

Through the centuries men have displayed many different symbols to show that they are Christians. They have worn marks in the lapels of their coats, hung chains about their necks, even had special haircuts.

Of course, there is nothing wrong with any of this, if one feels it is his calling. But there is a much better sign—a mark that has not been thought up just as a matter of expediency for use on some special occasion or in some specific era. It is a universal mark that is to last through all the ages of the church till Jesus comes back.

What is this mark?

At the close of his ministry, Jesus looks forward to his death on the cross, the open tomb and the ascension. Knowing that he is about to leave, Jesus prepares his disciples for what is to come. It is here that he makes clear what will be the distinguishing mark of the Christian:

> Little children, yet a little while I am with you. Ye shall
> seek me; and as I said unto the Jews, Whither I go, ye
> cannot come; so now I say to you. A new command-
> ment I give unto you, That ye love one another; as I
> have loved you, that ye also love one another. By this
> shall all men know that ye are my disciples, if ye have
> love one to another. (John 13:33-35)

This passage reveals the mark that Jesus gives to label a Christian not just in one era or in one locality but at all times and
all places until Jesus returns.

Notice that what he says here is not a description of a fact.
It is a command which includes a condition: "A new commandment I give unto you, That ye love one another; as I have
loved you, so ye love one another that all men know that ye
are my disciples, *if* ye have love one to another." An *if* is
involved. If you obey, you will wear the badge Christ gave. But
since this is a command, it can be violated.

The point is that it is possible to be a Christian without
showing the mark, but if we expect non-Christians to know
that we are Christians, we must show the mark.

men and brothers

The command at this point is to love our fellow Christians, our
brothers. But, of course, we must strike a balance and not
forget the other side of Jesus' teaching: We are to love our
fellowmen, to love *all* men, in fact, as neighbors.

All men bear the image of God. They have value, not because they are redeemed, but because they are God's creation
in God's image. Modern man, who has rejected this, has no
clue as to who he is, and because of this he can find no real
value for himself or for other men. Hence, he downgrades the
value of other men and produces the horrible thing we face

today—a sick culture in which men treat men as inhuman, as machines. As Christians, however, we know the value of men.

All men are our neighbors, and we are to love them as ourselves. We are to do this on the basis of creation, even if they are not redeemed, for all men have value because they are made in the image of God. Therefore they are to be loved even at great cost.

This is, of course, the whole point of Jesus' story of the good Samaritan: Because a man is a man, he is to be loved at all cost.

So, when Jesus gives the special command to love our Christian brothers, it does not negate the other command. The two are not antithetical. We are not to choose between loving all men as ourselves and loving the Christian in a special way. The two commands reinforce each other.

If Jesus has commanded so strongly that we love all men as our neighbors, then how important it is especially to love our fellow Christians. If we are told to love all men as our neighbors—as ourselves—then surely, when it comes to those with whom we have the special bonds as fellow Christians—having one Father through one Jesus Christ and being indwelt by one Spirit—we can understand how overwhelmingly important it is that all men be able to see an observable love for those with whom we have these special ties. Paul makes the double obligation clear in Galatians 6:10: "As we have therefore opportunity, let us do good unto all men, especially unto them who are of the household of faith." He does not negate the command to do good to all men. But it is still not meaningless to add, "especially unto them who are of the household of faith." This dual goal should be our Christian mentality, the set of our minds; we should be consciously thinking about it and what it means in our one-moment-at-a-time lives. It should be the attitude that governs our outward observable actions.

Very often the true Bible-believing Christian, in his emphasis on two humanities—one lost, one saved—one still standing in rebellion against God, the other having returned to God through Christ—has given a picture of exclusiveness which is ugly.

There are two humanities. That is true. Some men made in the image of God still stand in rebellion against him; some, by the grace of God, have cast themselves upon God's solution.

Nonetheless, there is in another very important sense only one humanity. All men derive from one origin. By creation all men bear the image of God. In this sense all men are of one flesh, one blood.

Hence, the exclusiveness of the two humanities is undergirded by the unity of all men. And Christians are not to love their believing brothers to the exclusion of their non-believing fellowmen. That is ugly. We are to have the example of the good Samaritan consciously in mind at all times.

a delicate balance

The first commandment is to love the Lord our God with all our heart, soul and mind. The second commandment bears the universal command to love men. Notice that the second commandment is not just to love Christians. It is far wider than this. We are to love our neighbor as ourselves.

I Thessalonians 3:12 carries the same double emphasis: "And the Lord make you to increase and abound in love one toward another, and toward all men, even as we do toward you." Here the order is reversed. First of all, we are to have love one toward another and then toward all men, but that does not change the double emphasis. Rather, it points up the delicate balance—a balance that is not in practice automatically maintained.

In I John 3:11 (written later than the gospel that bears his name) John says, "For this is the message that ye heard from the beginning, that we should love one another." Years after Christ's death, John, in writing the epistle, calls us back to Christ's original command in John 13. Speaking to the church, John in effect says, "Don't forget this . . . Don't forget this. This command was given to us by Christ while he was still on the earth. This is to be your mark."

for true christians only

If we look again at the command in John 13, we will notice some important things. First of all, this is a command to have a special love to all true Christians, all born-again Christians. From the scriptural viewpoint, not all who call themselves Christians are Christians, and that is especially true in our generation. The meaning of the word *Christian* has been reduced to practically nothing. Surely, there is no word that has been so devalued unless it is the word of God itself. Central to semantics is the idea that a word as a symbol has no meaning until content is put into it. This is quite correct. Because the word *Christian* as a symbol has been made to mean so little, it has come to mean everything and nothing.

Jesus, however, is talking about loving all true Christians. And this is a command that has two cutting edges, for it means that we must both distinguish true Christians from all pretenders and be sure that we leave no true Christians outside of our consideration. In other words, mere humanists and liberal theologians who continue to use the Christian label or mere church members whose Christian designation is only a formality are not to be accounted true.

But we must be careful of the opposite error. We must include *everyone* who stands in the historic-biblical faith whether or not he is a member of our own party or our own group.

But even if a man is not among the true Christians, we still have the responsibility to love him as our neighbor. So we cannot say, "Now here's somebody that, as far as I can tell, does not stand among the group of true Christians, and therefore I don't have to think of him any more; I can just slough him off." Not at all. He is covered by the second commandment.

the standard of quality

The second thing to notice in these verses in John 13 is the quality of the love that is to be our standard. We are to love all Christians "as I," Jesus says, "have loved you." Now think of both the quality and the quantity of Jesus' love toward us. Of course, he is infinite and we are finite; he is God, we are men. Since he is infinite, our love can never be like his, it can never be an infinite love.

Nevertheless, the love he exhibited then and exhibits now is to be our standard. We dare have no lesser standard. We are to love all true Christians as Christ has loved us.

Now immediately, when we say this, either of two things can happen. We can just say, "I see! I see!" and we can make a little flag and write on it, "We Love All Christians!" You can see us trudging along with little flags—all rolled up—"We Love All Christians!"—and at the appropriate moment, we take off all the rubber bands, unzip the cover, and put it up. We wave it as we carry it along—"We Love All Christians!" How ugly!

It can be either this exceedingly ugly thing, as ugly as anything anyone could imagine, or it can be something as profound as anyone could imagine. And if it is to be the latter, it will take a great deal of time, a great deal of conscious talking and writing about it, a great deal of thinking and praying about it on the part of the Bible-believing Christians.

The church is to be a loving church in a dying culture. How, then, is the dying culture going to consider us? Jesus says, "By this shall all men know that ye are my disciples, if ye have love one to another." In the midst of the world, in the midst of our present dying culture, Jesus is giving a right to the world. Upon his authority he gives the world the right to judge whether you and I are born-again Christians on the basis of our observable love toward all Christians.

That's pretty frightening. Jesus turns to the world and says, "I've something to say to you. On the basis of my authority, I give you a right: you may judge whether or not an individual is a Christian on the basis of the love he shows to all Christians." In other words, if people come up to us and cast in our teeth the judgment that we are not Christians because we have not shown love toward other Christians, we must understand that they are only exercising a prerogative which Jesus gave them.

And we must not get angry. If people say, "You don't love other Christians," we must go home, get down on our knees and ask God whether or not they are right. And if they are, then they have a right to have said what they said.

failure in love

We must be very careful at this point, however. We may be true Christians, really born-again Christians, and yet fail in our love toward other Christians. As a matter of fact, to be completely realistic, it is stronger than this. There will be times (and let us say it with tears), there will be times when we will fail in our love toward each other as Christians. In a fallen world, where there is no such thing as perfection until Jesus comes, we know this will be the case. And, of course, when we fail, we must ask God's forgiveness. But, Jesus is not here saying that our failure to love all Christians proves that we are not Christians.

Let each of us see this individually for ourselves. If I fail in my love toward Christians, it does not prove I am not a Christian. What Jesus is saying, however, is that, if I do not have the love I should have toward all other Christians, the world has the right to make the judgment that I am not a Christian.

This distinction is imperative. If we fail in our love toward all Christians, we must not tear our heart out as though it were proof that we are lost. No one except Christ himself has ever lived and not failed. If success in love toward our brothers in Christ were to be the standard of whether or not a man is a Christian, then there would be no Christians, because all men have failed. But Jesus gives the world a piece of litmus paper, a reasonable thermometer: There is a mark which, if the world does not see, allows them to conclude, "This man is not a Christian." Of course, the world may be making a wrong judgment because, if the man is truly a Christian, as far as the reality goes, they made a mistake.

It is true that a non-Christian often hides behind what he sees in Christians and then screams, "Hypocrites!" when in reality he is a sinner who will not face the claims of Christ. But that is not what Jesus is talking about here. Here Jesus is talking about our responsibility as individuals and as groups to so love all other true Christians that the world will have no valid reason for saying that we are not Christians.

the final apologetic

But there is something even more sober. And to understand it we must look at John 17:21, a verse out of the midst of Christ's high priestly prayer. Jesus prays, "That they all may be one; as thou, Father, art in me, and I in thee, that they also may be one in us; that the world may believe that thou hast sent me." In this, his high priestly prayer, Jesus is praying for the oneness of the church, the oneness that should be found specifically among true Christians. Jesus is not praying for a humanistic, romantic oneness among men in general. Verse 9 makes this clear: "I pray not for the world, but for them which thou hast given me; for they are thine." Jesus here makes a very careful distinction between those who have cast themselves upon him in faith and those who still stand in rebellion. Hence, in the 21st verse, when he prays for oneness, the "they" he is referring to are the true Christians.

Notice, however, that verse 21 says, "That they all may be one. . . ." The emphasis, interestingly enough, is exactly the same as in John 13—not on a part of true Christians, but on all Christians—not that those in certain parties in the church should be one, but that all born-again Christians should be one.

Now comes the sobering part. Jesus goes on in this 21st verse to say something that always causes me to cringe. If as Christians we do not cringe, it seems to me we are not very sensitive or very honest, because Jesus here gives us the final apologetic. What is the final apologetic? *"That they all may be one;* as thou, Father, art in me, and I in thee, that they also may be one in us: *that the world may believe that thou hast sent me."* This is the final apologetic.

In John 13 the point was that, if an individual Christian does not show love toward other true Christians, the world has a right to judge that he is not a Christian. Here Jesus is stating something else which is much more cutting, much more profound: We cannot expect the world to believe that the Father sent the Son, that Jesus' claims are true, and that Christianity is true, unless the world sees some reality of the oneness of true Christians.

Now that is frightening. Should we not feel some emotion at this point?

Look at it again. Jesus is not saying that Christians should judge each other (as to their being Christian or not) on this basis. Please notice this with tremendous care. The church is to judge whether a man is a Christian on the basis of his doctrine, the propositional content of his faith, and then his credible profession of faith. When a man comes before a local church that is doing its job, he will be quizzed on the content of what he believes. If, for example, a church is conducting a heresy trial (the New Testament indicates there are to be heresy trials in the church of Christ), the question of heresy will turn on the content of the man's doctrine. The church has a right to judge, in fact it is commanded to judge, a man on the content of what he believes and teaches.

But we cannot expect the world to judge that way, because the world cares nothing about doctrine. And that is especially true in the second half of the 20th century when, on the basis of their epistomology, men no longer believe even in the possibility of absolute truth. And if we are surrounded by a world which no longer believes in the concept of truth, certainly we cannot expect people to have any interest in whether a man's doctrine is correct or not.

But Jesus did give the mark that will arrest the attention of the world, even the attention of the modern man who says he is just a machine. Because every man is made in the image of God and has, therefore, aspirations for love, there is something that can be in every geographical climate—in every point of time—which cannot fail to arrest his attention.

What is it? The love that true Christians show for each other and not just for their own party.

honest answers, observable love

Of course as Christians we must not minimize the need to give honest answers to honest questions. We should have an intellectual apologetic. The Bible commands it and Christ and Paul exemplify it. In the synagogue, in the marketplace, in homes and in almost every conceivable kind of situation, Jesus and Paul discussed Christianity. It is likewise the Christian's task to be able to give an honest answer to an honest question and then to give it.

Yet, without true Christians loving one another, Christ says the world cannot be expected to listen, even when we give proper answers. Let us be careful, indeed, to spend a lifetime studying to give honest answers. For years the orthodox, evangelical church has done this very poorly. So it is well to spend time learning to answer the questions of men who are about us. But after we have done our best to communicate to a lost world, still we must never forget that the final apologetic which Jesus gives is the observable love of true Christians for true Christians.

While it is not the central consideration that I am dealing with at this time, yet the observable love and oneness among true Christians exhibited before the world must certainly cross all the lines which divide men. The New Testament says, "Neither Greek nor barbarian, neither Jew nor Gentile, neither male nor female."

In the church at Antioch the Christians included Jews and Gentiles and reached all the way from Herod's foster brother to the slaves; and the naturally proud Greek Christian Gentiles of Macedonia showed a practical concern for the material needs of the Christian Jews in Jerusalem. The observable and practical love among true Christians that the world has a right to be able to observe in our day certainly should cut without reservation across such lines as language, nationalities, national frontiers, younger and older, colors of skin, levels of education and economics, accent, line of birth, the class system in any particular locality, dress, short or long hair among whites and African and non-African hairdos among blacks, the wearing of shoes and the non-wearing of shoes, cultural differentiations and the more traditional and less traditional forms of worship.

If the world does not see this, it will not believe that Christ was sent by the Father. People will not believe only on the basis of the proper answers. The two should not be placed in antithesis. The world must have the proper answers to their honest questions, but at the same time, there must be a oneness in love between all true Christians. This is what is needed if men are to know that Jesus was sent by the Father and that Christianity is true.

false notions of unity

Let us be clear, however, about what this oneness is. We can start by eliminating some false notions. First, the oneness that Jesus is talking about is not just organizational oneness. In our generation we have a tremendous push for ecclesiastical oneness. It is in the air—like German measles in a time of epidemic—and it is all about us. Human beings can have all sorts of organizational unity but exhibit to the world no unity at all.

The classic example is the Roman Catholic Church down through the ages. The Roman Catholic Church has had a great external unity—probably the greatest outward organizational unity that has ever been seen in this world, but there have been at the same time titanic and hateful power struggles between the different orders within the one church. Today there is a still greater difference between the classical Roman Catholicism and progressive Roman Catholicism. The Roman Catholic Church still tries to stand in organizational oneness, but there is only organizational unity, for here are two completely different religions, two different concepts of God, two different concepts of truth.

And exactly the same thing is true in the Protestant ecumenical movement. There is an attempt to bring people together organizationally on the basis of Jesus' statement, but there is no real unity, because two completely different religions—biblical Christianity and a "Christianity" which is no Christianity whatsoever—are involved. It is perfectly possible to have organizational unity, to spend a whole lifetime of energy on it, and yet to come nowhere near the realm that Jesus is talking about in John 17.

I do not wish to disparage proper organizational unity on a proper doctrinal basis. But Jesus is here talking about something very different, for there can be a great organizational unity without any oneness at all—even in churches that have fought for purity.

I believe very strongly in the principle and practice of the purity of the visible church, but I have seen churches that have fought for purity and are merely hotbeds of ugliness. No longer is there any observable, loving, personal relationship even in their own midst, let alone with other true Christians.

There is a further reason why one cannot interpret this unity of which Christ speaks as organizational. *All* Christians— "That they all may be one"—are to be one. It is obvious that there can be no organizational unity which could include all born-again Christians everywhere in the world. It is just not possible. For example, there are true, born-again Christians who belong to no organization at all. And what one organization could include those true Christians standing isolated from the outside world by persecution? Obviously organizational unity is not the answer.

There is a second false notion of what this unity involves. This is the view that evangelical Christians have often tried to escape under. Too often the evangelical has said, "Well, of course Jesus is talking here about the mystical union of the invisible church." And then he lets it go at that and does not think about it any more—ever.

In theological terms there are, to be sure, a visible church and an invisible church. The invisible Church is the real Church—in a way, the only church that has a right to be spelled with a capital. Because it is made up of all those who have thrown themselves upon Christ as Savior, it is most important. It is Christ's Church. As soon as I become a Christian, as soon as I throw myself upon Christ, I become a member of this Church, and there is a mystical unity binding me to all other members. True. But this is not what Jesus is talking about in John 13 and John 17, for we cannot break up this unity no matter what we do. Thus, to relate Christ's words to the mystical unity of the invisible Church is to reduce Christ's words to a meaningless phrase.

Third, he is not talking about our positional unity in Christ. It is true that there is a positional unity in Christ—that as soon as we accept Christ as Savior we have one Lord, one baptism, one birth (the second birth), and we are clothed with Christ's righteousness. But that is not the point here.

Fourth, we have legal unity in Christ, but he is not talking about that. There is a beautiful and wonderful legal unity among all Christians. The Father (the judge of the universe) forensically declares, on the basis of the finished work of Christ in space, time and history, that the true moral guilt of those who cast themselves upon Christ is gone. In that fact we have a wonderful unity; but that is not what Jesus is talking about here.

It will not do for the evangelical to try to escape into the concept of the invisible Church and these other related unities. To relate these verses in John 13 and 17 merely to the existence of the invisible Church makes Jesus' statement a nonsense statement. We make a mockery of what Jesus is saying unless we understand that he is talking about something visible.

This is the whole point: The world is going to judge whether Jesus has been sent by the Father on the basis of something that is open to observation.

true oneness

In John 13 and 17, Jesus talks about a real seeable oneness, a practicing oneness, a practical oneness across all lines, among all true Christians.

The Christian really has a double task. He has to practice both God's holiness and God's love. The Christian is to exhibit that God exists as the infinite-personal God; and then he is to exhibit simultaneously God's character of holiness and love. Not his holiness without his love: that is only harshness. Not his love without his holiness: that is only compromise. Anything that an individual Christian or Christian group does that fails to show the simultaneous balance of the holiness of God and the love of God presents to a watching world not a demonstration of the God who exists but a caricature of the God who exists.

According to the Scripture and the teaching of Christ, the love that is shown is to be exceedingly strong. It is not just something you mention in words once in a while.

visible love

What, then, does this love mean? How can it be made visible?

First, it means a very simple thing: It means that when I have made a mistake and when I have failed to love my Christian brother, I go to him and say, "I'm sorry." That is first.

It may seem a letdown—that the first thing we speak of should be so simple! But if you think it is easy, you have never tried to practice it.

In our own groups, in our own close Christian communities, even in our families, when we have shown lack of love toward

21

another, we as Christians do not just automatically go and say we are sorry. On even the very simplest level it is never very easy.

It may sound simplistic to start with saying we are sorry and asking forgiveness, but it is not. This is the way of renewed fellowship, whether it is between a husband and wife, a parent and child, within a Christian community, or between groups. When we have shown a lack of love toward the other, we are called by God to go and say, "I'm sorry. . . . I really am sorry."

If I am not willing to say, "I'm sorry," when I have wronged somebody else—especially when I have not loved him—I have not even started to think about the meaning of a Christian oneness which the world can see. The world has a right to question whether I am a Christian. And more than that, let me say it again, if I am not willing to do this very simple thing, the world has a right to question whether Jesus was sent from God and whether Christianity is true.

How well have we consciously practiced this? How often, in the power of the Holy Spirit, have we gone to Christians in our own group and said,"I'm sorry"? How much time have we spent reestablishing contact with those in other groups, saying to them, "I'm sorry for what I've done, what I've said, or what I've written"? How frequently has one *group* gone to another *group* with whom it differed and has said, "We're sorry"? It is so important that it is, for all practical purposes, a part of the preaching of the gospel itself. The observable practice of truth and the observable practice of love go hand in hand with the proclamation of the good news of Jesus Christ.

I have observed one thing *among true Christians* in their differences in many countries: What divides and severs true Christian groups and Christians—what leaves a bitterness that can last for 20, 30 or 40 years (or for 50 or 60 years in a son's memory)—is not the issue of doctrine or belief which caused the differences in the first place. Invariably it is lack of love—and the bitter things that are said by true Christians in the midst of differences. These stick in the mind like glue. And after time passes and the differences between the Christians or the groups appear less than they did, there are still those bitter, bitter things we said in the midst of what we thought was a good and sufficient objective discussion. It is these things—these unloving attitudes and words—that cause the stench that the world can smell in the church of Jesus Christ among those who are really true Christians.

If, when we feel we must disagree as true Christians, we could simply guard our tongues and speak in love, in five or ten years the bitterness could be gone. Instead of that, we leave scars—a curse for generations. Not just a curse in the church, but a curse in the world. Newspaper headlines bear it in our Christian press, and it boils over into the secular press at times—Christians saying such bitter things about other Christians.

The world looks, shrugs its shoulders and turns away. It has not seen even the beginning of a living church in the midst of a dying culture. It has not seen the beginning of what Jesus indicates is the final apologetic—observable oneness among true Christians who are truly brothers in Christ. Our sharp tongues, the lack of love between us—not the necessary statements of differences that may exist between true Christians—these are what properly trouble the world.

How different this is from the straightforward and direct command of Jesus Christ—to show an observable oneness which may be seen by a watching world!

forgiveness
But there is more to observable love than saying we are sorry.

There must also be open forgiveness. And though it's hard to say, "I'm sorry," it's even harder to forgive. The Bible, however, makes plain that the world must observe a forgiving spirit in the midst of God's people.

In the Lord's prayer, Jesus himself teaches us to pray, "Forgive us our trespasses, as we forgive those who trespass against us." Now this prayer, we must say quickly, is not for salvation. It has nothing to do with being born again, for we are born again on the basis of the finished work of Christ plus nothing. But it does have to do with a Christian's existential, moment-by-moment experiential relationship to God. We need a once-for-all forgiveness at justification, and we need a moment-by-moment forgiveness for our sins on the basis of Christ's work in order to be in open fellowship with God. What the Lord has taught us to pray in the Lord's prayer should make a Christian very sober every day of his life: We are asking the Lord to open to us the experiential realities of fellowship with himself as we forgive others.

Some Christians say that the Lord's prayer is not for this present era, but most of us would say it is. And yet at the same time we hardly think once in a year about our lack of a forgiving heart in relationship to God's forgiving us. Many Christians rarely or never seem to connect their own lack of reality of fellowship with God with their lack of forgiveness to men, even though they may say the Lord's prayer in a formal way over and over in their weekly Sunday worship services.

We must all continually acknowledge that we do not practice the forgiving heart as we should. And yet the prayer is "Forgive us our debts, our trespasses, as we forgive our debtors." We are to have a forgiving spirit even before the other person expresses regret for his wrong. The Lord's prayer does not suggest that when the other man is sorry, then we are to show a oneness by having a forgiving spirit. Rather, we are

called upon to have a forgiving spirit without the other man
having made the first step. We may still say that he is wrong,
but in the midst of saying that he is wrong, we must be forgiving.

We are to have this forgiving spirit not only toward Christians but toward all men. But surely if it is toward all men, it is
important toward Christians.

Such a forgiving spirit registers an attitude of love toward
others. But, even though one can call this an attitude, true
forgiveness is observable. Believe me, you can look on a man's
face and know where he is as far as forgiveness is concerned.
And the world is called on to look upon us and see whether we
have love across the groups, love across party lines. Do they
observe that we say, "I'm sorry," and do they observe a forgiving heart? Let me repeat: Our love will not be perfect, but
it must be substantial enough for the world to be able to
observe or it does not fit into the structure of the verses in
John 13 and 17. And if the world does not observe this among
true Christians, the world has a right to make the two awful
judgments which these verses indicate: That we are not Christians and that Christ was not sent by the Father.

when christians disagree

What happens, then, when we must differ with other brothers
in Christ because of the need also to show forth God's holiness
either in doctrine or in life? In the matter of life, Paul clearly
shows us the balance in I and II Corinthians. The same thing
applies in doctrine as well.

First, in I Corinthians 5:1-5 he scolds the Corinthian church
for allowing a man in the midst of fornication to stay in the
church without discipline. Because of the holiness of God,
because of the need to exhibit this holiness to a watching
world, and because such judgment on the basis of God's re-

vealed law is right in God's sight, Paul scolds the church for not disciplining the man.

After they have disciplined him, Paul writes again to them in II Corinthians 2:6-8 and scolds them because they are not showing love toward him. These two things must stand together.

I am thankful that Paul writes this way in his first letter and his second, for here you see a passage of time. The Corinthians have taken his advice, they have disciplined the Christian, and now Paul writes to them, "You're disciplining him, but why don't you show your love toward him?" He could have gone on and quoted Jesus in saying, "Don't you realize that the surrounding pagans of Corinth have a right to say that Jesus was not sent by the Father because you are not showing love to this man that you properly disciplined?"

A very important question arises at this point: How can we exhibit the oneness Christ commands without sharing in the other man's mistakes? I would suggest a few ways by which we can practice and show this oneness even across the lines where we must differ.

regret

First, we should never come to such difference with true Christians without regret and without tears. Sounds simple, doesn't it? Believe me, evangelicals often have not shown it. We rush in, being very, very pleased, it would seem at times, to find other men's mistakes. We build ourselves up by tearing other men down. This can never show a real oneness among Christians.

There is only one kind of man who can fight the Lord's battles in anywhere near a proper way, and that is the man who by nature is unbelligerent. A belligerent man tends to do it because he is belligerent; at least it looks that way. The world must observe that, when we must differ with each other as true Christians, we do it not because we love the smell of blood, the smell of the arena, the smell of the bullfight, but because we must for God's sake. If there are tears when we must speak, then something beautiful can be observed.

Second, in proportion to the gravity of what is wrong between true Christians, it is important consciously to exhibit a seeable love to the world. Not all differences among Christians are equal. There are some that are very minor. Others are overwhelmingly important.

The more serious the wrongness is, the more important it is to exhibit the holiness of God, to speak out concerning what is wrong. At the same time, the more serious the differences become, the more important it becomes that we look to the Holy Spirit to enable us to show love to the true Christians with whom we must differ. If it is only a minor difference, showing love does not take much conscious consideration. But where the difference becomes really important, it becomes proportionately more important to speak for God's holiness. And it becomes increasingly important in that place to show the world that we still love each other.

Humanly we function in exactly the opposite direction: In the less important differences we show more love toward true Christians, but as the difference gets into more important areas, we tend to show less love. The reverse must be the case: As the differences among true Christians get greater, we must *consciously* love and show a love which has some manifestation the world may see.

So let us consider this: Is my difference with my brother in Christ really crucially important? If so, it is doubly important that I spend time upon my knees asking the Holy Spirit, asking Christ, to do his work through me and my group, that I and we might show love even in this larger difference that we have come to with a brother in Christ or with another group of true Christians.

costly love

Third, we must show a *practical* demonstration of love in the midst of the dilemma even when it is costly. The word *love* should not be just a banner. In other words, we must do whatever must be done, at whatever cost, to show this love. We must not say, "I love you," and then—bang, bang, bang!

So often people think that Christianity is only something soft, only a kind of gooey love that loves evil equally with good. This is not the biblical position. The holiness of God is to be exhibited simultaneously with love. We must be careful therefore, not to say that what is wrong is right, whether it is in the area of doctrine or of life, in our own group or another. Anywhere what is wrong is wrong, and we have a responsibility in that situation to say that what is wrong is wrong. But the observable love must be there regardless of the cost.

The Bible does not make these things escapable. I Corinthians 6:1-7 reads,

Dare any of you, having a matter against another, go to law before the unjust [that is, the unsaved people], and not before the saints? Do ye not know that the saints shall judge the world? and if the world shall be judged by you, are ye unworthy to judge the smallest matters? Know ye not that we shall judge angels? how much more things that pertain to this life? If then ye have judgments of things pertaining to this life, set them to judge who are least esteemed in the church. I speak to your shame. Is it so, that there is not a wise man among you? no, not one that shall be able to judge between his brethren? But brother goeth to law with brother, and that before the unbelievers. Now therefore there is utterly a fault among you, because ye go to law one with another. *Why do ye not rather take wrong? Why do ye not rather suffer yourselves to be defrauded?*

What does this mean? The church is not to let pass what is wrong; but the Christian should suffer practical, monetary loss to show the oneness true Christians should have rather than to go to court against other true Christians, for this would destroy such an observable oneness before the watching world. This is costly love, but it is just such practicing love that can be seen.

Paul is talking about something which is observable, something that is very real: The Christian is to show such love in the midst of a necessary difference with his brother that he is willing to suffer loss—not just monetary loss (though most Christians seem to forget all love and oneness when money gets involved) but whatever loss is involved.

Whatever the specifics are, there is to be a practical demonstration of love appropriate to a particular place. The Bible is a strong and down-to-earth book.

A fourth way we can show and exhibit love without sharing in our brother's mistake is to approach the problem with a desire to solve it, rather than with a desire to win. We all love to win. In fact, there is nobody who loves to win more than the theologian. The history of theology is all too often a long exhibition of a desire to win.

But we should understand that what we are working for in the midst of our difference is a *solution* —a solution that will give God the glory, that will be true to the Bible, but will exhibit the love of God simultaneously with his holiness. What is our attitude as we sit down to talk to our brother or as group meets with group to discuss differences? A desire to come out on top? To play one-up-manship? If there is any desire for love whatsoever, every time we discuss a difference, we will desire a solution and not just that we can be proven right.

the difference of differences

A fifth way in which we can show a practicing, observable love to the world without sharing in our brother's mistake is to realize, to keep *consciously* before us and to help each other be aware, that it is easy to compromise and to call what is wrong right, but that it is equally easy to forget to exhibit our oneness in Christ. This attitude must be constantly and consciously developed—talked about and written about in and among our groups and among ourselves as individuals.

In fact, this must be talked about and written about *before* differences arise between true Christians. We have conferences about everything else. Who has ever heard of a conference to consider how true Christians can exhibit in practice a fidelity to the holiness of God and yet simultaneously exhibit in practice a fidelity to the love of God before a watching world? Whoever heard of sermons or writings which carefully present the practice of two principles which at first seem to work against each other: (1) the principle of the practice of the purity of the visible church in regard to doctrine and life and (2) the principle of the practice of an observable love and oneness among *all* true Christians?

If there is no careful preaching and writing about these things, are we so foolish as to think that there will be anything beautiful in practice when differences between true Christians must honestly be faced?

Before a watching world an observable love in the midst of difference will show a difference between Christians' differences and other men's differences. The world may not understand what the Christians are disagreeing about, but they will very quickly understand the difference of our differences from the world's differences if they see us having our differences in an open and observable love on a practical level.

That *is* different. Can you see why Jesus said this was the thing that would arrest the attention of the world? You cannot expect the world to understand doctrinal differences, especially in our day when the existence of true truth and absolutes are considered unthinkable even as concepts.

We cannot expect the world to understand that on the basis of the holiness of God we are having a different kind of difference because we are dealing with God's absolutes. But when they see differences among true Christians who also show an observable unity, this will open the way for them to consider the truth of Christianity and Christ's claim that the Father did send the Son.

As a matter of fact, we have a greater possibility of showing what Jesus is speaking about here in the midst of our differences, than we do if we are not differing. Obviously we ought not to go out looking for differences among Christians: There are enough without looking for more. But even so it is in the midst of a difference that we have our golden opportunity. When everything is going well and we are all standing around in a nice little circle, there is not much to be seen by the world. But when we come to the place where there is a real difference and we exhibit uncompromised principles but at the same time observable love, then there is something that the world can see, something they can use to judge that these really are Christians, and that Jesus has indeed been sent by the Father.

love in practice
Let me give two beautiful examples of such observable love. One happened among the Brethren groups in Germany immediately after the last war.

In order to control the church, Hitler commanded the union of all religious groups in Germany, drawing them together by law. The Brethren divided over this issue. Half accepted Hitler's dictum and half refused. The ones who submitted, of course, had a much easier time, but gradually in this organizational oneness with the liberal groups their own doctrinal sharpness and spiritual life withered. On the other hand, the group that stayed out remained spiritually virile, but there was hardly a family in which someone did not die in a German concentration camp.

Now can you imagine the emotional tension? The war is over, and these Christian brothers face each other again. They had the same doctrine and they had worked together for more than a generation. Now what is going to happen? One man remembers that his father died in a concentration camp and knows that these people over here remained safe. But people on the other side have deep personal feelings as well.

Then gradually these brothers came to know that this situation just would not do. A time was appointed when the elders of the two groups could meet together in a certain quiet place. I asked the man who told me this, "What did you do?" And he said, "Well, I'll tell you what we did. We came together, and we set aside several days in which each man would search his own heart." Here was a real difference; the emotions were deeply, deeply stirred. "My father has gone to the concentration camp; my mother was dragged away." These things are not just little pebbles on the beach; they reach into the deep wellsprings of human emotions. But these people understood the command of Christ at this place, and for several days every man did nothing except search his own heart concerning his own failures and the commands of Christ. Then they met together.

I asked the man, "What happened then?"

And he said, "We just were one."

To my mind, this is exactly what Jesus speaks about. The Father has sent the Son!

divided but one

The principle we are talking about is universal, applicable in all times and places. Let me, then, give you a second illustration—a different practice of the same principle.

I have been waiting for years for a time when two groups of born-again Christians who for good reasons find it impossible to work together separate without saying bitter things against each other. I have long longed for two groups who would continue to show a love to the watching world when they came to the place where organizational unity seemed no longer possible between them.

Theoretically, of course, every local church ought to be able to minister to the whole spectrum of society. But in practice we must acknowledge that in certain places it becomes very difficult. The needs of different segments of society are different.

Recently a problem of this nature arose in a church in a large city in the Midwest in the United States. A number of people attuned to the modern age were going to a certain church, but the pastor gradually concluded that he was not able to preach and minister to the two groups. Some men can, but he personally did not find it possible to minister to the whole spectrum of his congregation—the long-haired ones and the far-out people they brought, and, at the same time, the people of the surrounding neighborhood.

The example of observable love I am going to present now must not be taken as an "of course" situation in our day. In our generation the lack of love can easily cut both ways: A middle-class people can all too easily be snobbish and unloving

33

against the long-haired Christians, and the long-haired Christians can be equally snobbish and unloving against the short-haired Christians.

After trying for a long time to work together, the elders met and decided that they would make two churches. They made it very plain that they were not dividing because their doctrine was different; they were dividing as a matter of practicability. One member of the old session went to the new group. They worked under the whole session to make an orderly transition. Now they have two churches and they are consciously practicing love toward each other.

Here is a lack of organizational unity that is a true love and unity which the world may observe. The Father has sent the Son!

I want to say with all my heart that as we struggle with the proper preaching of the gospel in the midst of the 20th century, the importance of observable love must come into our message. We must not forget the final apologetic. The world has a right to look upon us as we, as true Christians, come to practical differences and it should be able to observe that we do love each other. Our love must have a form that the world may observe; it must be seeable.

the one true mark

Let us look again at the biblical texts which so clearly indicate the mark of the Christian:

A new commandment I give unto you, That ye love one another; as I have loved you, that ye also love one another. By this shall all men know that ye are my disciples, if ye have love one to another. (John 13:34-35)

That they all may be one; as thou, Father, art in me, and I in thee, that they also may be one in us: that the world may believe that thou hast sent me. (John 17:21)

What then shall we conclude but that as the Samaritan loved the wounded man, we as Christians are called upon to love *all* men as neighbors, loving them as ourselves. Second, that we are to love all true Christian brothers in a way that the world may observe. This means showing love to our brothers in the midst of our differences—great or small—loving our brothers when it costs us something, loving them even under times of tremendous emotional tension, loving them in a way the world can see. In short, we are to practice and exhibit the holiness of God and the love of God, for without this we grieve the Holy Spirit.

Love—and the unity it attests to—is the mark Christ gave Christians to *wear* before the world. Only with this mark may the world know that Christians are indeed Christians and that Jesus was sent by the Father.

LAMENT

by Evangeline Paterson

Weep, weep for those
Who do the work of the Lord
With a high look
And a proud heart.
Their voice is lifted up
In the streets, and their cry is heard.
The bruised reed they break
By their great strength, and the smoking flax
They trample.

Weep not for the quenched
(For their God will hear their cry
And the Lord will come to save them)
But weep, weep for the quenchers

For when the Day of the Lord
Is come, and the vales sing
And the hills clap their hands
And the light shines

Then their eyes shall be opened
On a waste place,
Smouldering,
The smoke of the flax bitter
In their nostrils,
Their feet pierced
By broken reed-stems . . .
Wood, hay, and stubble,
And no grass springing,
And all the birds flown.

Weep, weep for those
Who have made a desert
In the name of the Lord.

From *Deep Is the Rock*
(Elms Court: Arthur H. Stockwell Limited, 1966).
© 1966 by *Christianity Today*.
Reprinted by permission.